Collected Winning Poems

from

The Poetry Society of Virginia

2022

Copyright © 2022 by The Poetry Society of Virginia.
All Rights Reserved
Individual copyrights are held by each author.
For a complete list, see the table of contents of the book.

Thank you for purchasing an authorized edition of *Collected Winning Poems from The Poetry Society of Virginia*

High Tide's mission is to find, encourage, promote, and publish the work of authors. We are a small, woman-owned enterprise that is dedicated to authors in all phases of their writing journey. When you buy an authorized copy, you help us to bring their work to you.

When you honor copyright law by not reproducing or scanning any part (in any form) without our written permission, you enable us to support authors, publish their work, and bring it to you to enjoy.

We thank you for supporting our authors.

ISBN: 978-1-945990-93-9

Cover Illustration by Terry Cox-Joseph
Credits: [126976664](#) © [Traci Vanover](#) | [Dreamstime.com](#),
Photo [186356297](#) / [Edgar Allan Poe](#) © [Sarah Richardson](#) | [Dreamstime.com](#),
Photo [151752769](#) © [Aleksandar Mijatovic](#) | [Dreamstime.com](#).

Congratulations to all the winners of the 2022 PSV Annual Poetry Contest! We are thrilled to present our yearly book of winners.

So, why publish a book of winning entries? Publishing not only validates poets, it gives others a sense of what wins. Having said that, we rarely use the same judges for the same categories. The standard is simple whether the poem is strong, not whether it is to the judge's taste.

The book is also entertaining, elucidating and useful as a work of its own. What sort of work shines? How to choose a theme? The Poe category is wide open. Others, such as the Bess Gresham Memorial, have a theme. Notes for future contests: if your poem did not place in any if the categories, you may resubmit it in a different category the following year.

We try our best to mix-and-match the judges. We are asking winners of any single contest to skip a year before submitting to that specific category again, to give others a chance to shine.

I hope that this volume will delight, awaken, and inspire you.

Terry Cox-Joseph, President, 2022
Poetry Society of Virginia

Categories and Winners

Category 1 - Edgar Allan Poe -
   1st Place *Everywhere the Rain is Falling Now* **Gail Giewont**   *1*
   2nd Place *Mayan Child* **Eric Forsbergh**   *2*

Category 2 - Sarah Lockwood Memorial -
   1st Place *Leaving the Homeplace: A Sonnet Sequence* **Chapman Hood Frazier**   *3*
   2nd Place *The Stalwart Toad, Italian sonnet* **Erin Newton Wells**   *6*

Category 3 - Bess Gresham Memorial -
   1st Place *A True Friend* **Edward Wright Haile**   *7*
   2nd Place *Hemerocallis (Daylily)* **Peter LaBerge**   *8*

Category 4 - Carleton Drewry Memorial -
   2nd Place *Mending the Shovel* **Erin Newton Wells**   *10*

Category 5 - Brodie Herndon Memorial -
   1st Place *Vigil* **Erin Newton Wells**   *11*
   2nd Place *Blueberry Hill* **Catherine West Johnson**   *12*

Category 6 - Nancy Byrd Turner Memorial -
   1st Place *Clearcut (A Clogyrnach)* **Elizabeth Spencer Spragins**   *14*
   2nd Place *Signs and Wonders (English sonnet)* **Erin Newton Wells**   *16*

Category 7 - Cenie H. Moon Prize -
   1st Place *A Mantle of Words* **Erin Newton Wells**   *17*
   2nd Place *Luminosity* **Chapman Hood Frazier**   *18*

Category 8 - Judah, Sarah, Grace, and Tom Memorial -
   1st Place *Didactic Haikus* **Richard L. Rose**   *19*
   2nd Place *Where the Ground Weeps* **Erin Newton Wells**   *20*

Category 9 - Ada Sanderson Memorial -
   1st Place *Elegy, Because the Season Does Not End* **Erin Newton Wells**   *22*
   2nd Place *Earth to Earth* **Gloria Williams Tran**   *23*

Category 10 - Charlotte Wise Memorial -
   1st Place *Easter Morning* **Chapman Hood Frazier**   *25*
   2nd Place *Home Studio* **Meg Eden**   *26*

Category 11 - Robert Sergeant Memorial -
   1st Place *City Birds* **Norma Cofresi**   *27*
   2nd Place *A Round of Robins* **Denise Wilcox**   *28*

Category 12 - Anne Spencer Memorial -
   1st Place *After My Husband Decides to Move in with a Woman He Met Last Week, I Take Myself Out to Lunch* **Gail Giewont**   *29*
   2nd Place *Call it Coping, Call it What You Will* **Mara Lee Grayson**   *30*

Category 13 - Handy Andy Prize -
   1st Place *Piccolo Practice* **Elizabeth Spencer Spraggins**   *32*
   2nd Place *Internal Combustion* **Richard L. Rose**   *33*

Category 14 - Alfred C. Gary Memorial -
  1st Place *This Day the Sea Will Boil* **Erin Newton Wells** 34
  2nd Place *At the Back of the March on the Pentagon, 1967* **Raymond Copson** 36

Category 15 - Laura Day Boggs Bolling Memorial -
  1st Place *To Catch Their Extravagant Wings* **Erin Newton Wells** 37
  2nd Place *Yodel for My Brother* **Laura Sweeney** 38

Category 16 - Joe Pendleton Campbell Memorial -
  1st Place *Asters Greet as They Pass While Faintly Smiling* **Cherryl Cooley** 39
  2nd Place *Badlands* **Maggie Dillow** 40

Category 17 - Dr. Lucile E. Thompson Memorial Award - Technology -
  1st Place *Ode for The Virtual Communities I Have Zoomed with This Year* **Laura Sweeney** 42
  2nd Place *An Underwood No. 5* **Erin Newton Wells** 43

Category 18 - Elizabeth J. Urquhart Memorial, A Sense of Place -
  1st Place *Ghosts Lights of Saratoga* **Erin Newton Wells** 44
  2nd Place *Visiting Danny* **Kathryn Paulsen** 45

Category 19 - The Joanne Scott Kennedy Memorial -
  1st Place *Candle Flame* **Claudia Serea** 46
  2nd Place *Fish Eyes* **Kaitlyn Graham** 47

Category 20 - Honoring Fatherhood Award -
  1st Place *All the Whens* **Stacy Clair** 48
  2nd Place *Breakers* **David Patteson** 50

Category 21 - Ekphrastic Poetry Award -
  1st Place *The Rose Window* **Chapman Hood Frazier** 51
  2nd Place *world of woe* **Rich Follett** 52

Category 22 - Emma Gray Trigg Memorial -
  1st Place *To Uncertainty* **Jay Udall** 54
  2nd Place *Blue Peony* **Peter C. LaBerge** 55

Category 23 - Karma Deane Ogden Memorial -
  1st Place *Hydrangeaphilia* **Gail Giewont** 57
  2nd Place *Jig* **Cherryl Cooley** 58

Category 24 - Loretta Dunn Hall Memorial -
  1st Place *Rose Tea* **Erin Newton Wells** 60
  2nd Place *Namesake* **Chapman Hood Frazier** 61

Category 25 - Undergraduate Poetry Award -
  1st Place *On a Sidewalk* **Alexander Lazarus Wolff** 62
  2nd Place *Apathy* **Ian Garrabrant** 63

Index by Poet 64

Category 1 - Edgar Allan Poe - 1st Place

Everywhere the Rain is Falling Now
Gail Giewont

It arrived at Aaliyah's house
first. Here, the skies were
silent, holding their breath.
An exhale: rain on the unopened
redbud blossoms, on violets
that litter the backyard, on the chickweed's
white flowers. As if rain can only fall
on what will bloom.

        There it is, too,
where the ice storm overweighted
the pine, its needles finally
browning, its body stiff
over the allium beds, over the buried bones
of my deaf white dog—where I should,
by now, have made space for the ashes
of the schnauzer the winter took.
I have, after all, been digging: rain puddles
where I planted the blueberry bush
that vanished, a hole in the ground
and no answer.

        Here, in my ribcage,
listen. Rain may always be there, gentle
or about to downpour, as if something
ought to grow there, or something ought
to drown.

Category 1 - Edgar Allan Poe - 2nd Place

Mayan Child
Eric Forsbergh

Coming here, we were lucky
to avoid
the soldiers on patrol.
Some mornings, fog shrouds the volcano.
Yet every day, the mountain retches smoke.

Long braids woven into closed loops,
Q'eqchi mothers
cluster in a tide of children.
Only today for this schoolyard.
Only today to triage and treat.

The girl's motionless eyes
can't help but notice my hands
as I barb the cartridge
into the syringe.

Her lips don't purse as I lean in.
Gingerly, my finger draws aside
her cheek for 25-gauge
injections
in the mouth.
Multiples, around
the abscessed teeth.

At four they thrash like wildcats.
By eight, she's learned when and how
to dull herself.
Her eyes fix on the pocked wall opposite:
Los Desaparecidos.
The words search door to door,
while in her lap,
her hands play dead.

Category 2 - Sarah Lockwood Memorial - 1ˢᵗ Place

Leaving the Homeplace: A Sonnet Sequence
Chapman Hood Frazier

Portrait beneath the Arbor

A four-year-old pushes her wicker baby
buggy with its blue-eyed doll towards father.
Her eight-year-old brother watches. He's
smelling a white rose. Behind them the arbor's
in full bloom. Each peace rose white and
fragrant even in shadow. These are the blooms
of late spring. The photographer sets
the aperture then raises his hand, a still life.

In a year, the son will die in an accident
and the father will suffer his first stroke.
The daughter will lay her doll down to sleep
in a house filling with the smoke of loss.
Only this portrait endures with white roses
a spring promise caught in sepia and gold.

During the Dying Time

A spring promise caught in sepia and gold
as each face smiles fresh with expectations.
By 1949 though, the house nearly empty.
Her daughter away at college and son gone
now fourteen years. Upstairs, her husband
barely breathing. What's to remember during
dying times? Slant of light across the morning
table, clink of spoon against the teacup

and by evening amber light through the window.
Street sounds fade away in what light remains.
She almost forgives him for not saving their son.
In the garden, roses dying too. Witches broom
reddens then twists the canes at the break of day
till they thorn-thicken then soften to decay.

Sarah Lockwood Memorial, Category 2 - 1ˢᵗ Place

Shedding the Shell

They thorn-thicken then soften to decay.
A hermit crab molts before shedding. Vulnerable,
a soul too must bury itself in the body's soil
before unraveling its soft self from its spiral
and search for a safe shell to believe in, something
soft and larger to protect itself and trust into
leaving behind the blue smoke of grief and
each glowing orange ember that turns to ash.

Each blind encumbrance crumbles gray and is soft
to the touch as it becomes a cross drawn on
each forehead at lent in the name of the father,
son and holy ghost. This, the gift of forgiveness
is the final chapter in *The Tibetan Book
of the Dead*, what's left is just loss of light.

The Promise

What's left is just a loss of light, each belief
in a sanctity of starlight. On the dorm
phone, she listens to her father gasping. His
breath whispering words heard but confused.
Instead, she imagines him behind his mahogany
desk, pipe in hand, white suit immaculate
and in his lapel, a blue bachelor button. This
is the image she treasures. By Christmas, she'll

bring home the man she'll marry to meet her
father on his deathbed. Father asks to be left alone
with him. "Promise me, you'll always protect her
even from herself. She's all I have left." By the
Christmas wedding, he'll be dead. But the promise
lasts like moss on a headstone, green and enduring.

Sarah Lockwood Memorial, Category 2 - 1st Place

The Spirit of the House

Like moss on a headstone, green and enduring
each memory softens with age. Years later, she returns
to sell her childhood home. Her grown sons wait
in the car, as she completes a final walk through. She

stops by her father's study remembering pipe smoke,
his white suit and flower the color of his eyes. Her great-
grandmother built the house passed down through
the motherline. How ironic that she has four sons who
will never live there. As she passes the music room towards
the door, a woman in black, hair coiled in a bun, stands
before the mantel. She stops, catches her breath and begins
to cry. The woman only turns her head to stare before
returning her gaze to the mirror. In the car, she is crying
as they drive away. Memory remains, all legacy in time.

Legacy

As they drive away, memory retains all legacy in time.
She tears up recalling his shadow from the headstone
cast and how the dead thorns thicken then soften
to decay and how each spring there is a promise
caught in sepia and gold of a four-year-old pushing
her wicker baby buggy in the portrait of the arbor
that rests on the mahogany table. What are these
shells shedding but promises the spirits keep alive.

From one generation to the next, legacy remains
in each broken moment when the light's right.
White as a peace rose blooming at noon or the
scent of pipe smoke in the green room as the blind
breaths from the cracked attic's window glass.
Each is a photograph fading white in the light.

Category 2 - Sarah Lockwood Memorial - 2nd Place

The Stalwart Toad, Italian sonnet
Erin Newton Wells

This is too horrible to tell, the day
the tilted stones are moved and set aside
to make a better path, the hole that hides
a toad revealed, the toad asleep, the way

its eyes are open when it sleeps, or may
have only briefly seen a black snake glide
from underneath a stack of stones beside
the hole to capture what is there and stay

all day ingesting it within sprung jaws,
the disappearing stalwart toad, its eyes
wide open, dead in part, or death is here

already so it does not piecemeal die,
a body slowly crushed. Let what I saw
not feel its death or see or know or fear.

Category 3 – Bess Gresham Memorial – 1st Place

A True Friend
Edward Wright Haile

A true friend is one alone
who can cuss me back on the straight road.
A woman once came between us,
I said to him. Yes, where is that woman now?
I believe she turned into the figurehead of ship.
Or became coins and someone else fought over her.
And we rambled out through open windows,
giving all our space to hills of grass.

Would a *friendsmith* work as in wood or metal?
I wondered in his direction,
and turning like a team he said no smith about it.
Rather the figure is rocks in a stream,
first loth then eager in tumbling
until they fit each other and bed.
We struggle forever to change shape, do we not?
Streams are faster to find us the shape of friends.
Now the woods approach.

Life's about two friends, seldom three.
More breaks off into a wife and a child,
and the staccato of things.
He'd read about a crowd of people
who veered this way and that, losing numbers,
until they trekked into the middle of somebody's set-to
and found themselves "allies of the winners."
That was the name they picked
to pronounce themselves a lucky race.
Then how come we, who share no blood in common,
are friends? And he turned like headsails aback,
looking just like an elf when he said
that friendship is not an accumulation or a circumstance,
nor is it to survive, or strike fortune.
It is the two-letter alphabet of all space.

Category 3 - Bess Gresham Memorial - 2nd Place

Hemerocallis (Daylily)
Peter LaBerge

You've filled each day I've visited this city
with every possibility of orange, wide blooms

I press between the pages of a book I open now
to visit the days I remember, the days I keep

remembering: *Golden Girls* reruns, the two of us

raining fine sugar into a glass bowl like fools, walking
down the street to pick up semi-sweet morsels

like I hadn't spent most of adulthood

so far in the rafters of my brain, watching my loneliness open
and close, open and close in the backyard: desire crackled

bug green in those days, heat lightning snaking
through the blooming rows, where it was anything

but wanted: I didn't know want, I only knew

I wanted to stop wanting: but now, I wake
smelling again like the thought

that opens you: a world of pollen welcoming you
into another morning as it comes.

Category 4 - Carleton Drewry Memorial - 1st Place

Place withdrawn from publication by submitter (Eric Forsbergh)

Category 4 - Carleton Drewry Memorial - 2nd Place

Mending the Shovel
Erin Newton Wells

The grain matters. He cuts the rivets, pushes them
from the neck, digs the broken shank
where it split after years of trenches and furrows,
the wood darkened in the pattern of his hands.
The new one, good ash, feels true. Slide the palm
on its length. Heft it, test it. Fit shoulder to head
with face grain to the sides for slack, its give
and take in the widening ovals, the rings of the tree.
Put the grain with straight lines beneath and on top.
He calls them the courage of the tree, its sinew
and muscle to bear the load and be part of him.
New rivets hold the shank and head. A sledge
knocks them in on one side. A ball-peen flattens
on the other. Sand the metal, bevel the edge, reset
the point to give it what years it lost. Oil them,
metal and wood, so the ash looks like clear honey.
These days he does not know my name sometimes.
Find the shovel in the shed, its honest scent.
Place it near his hand. A garden flourishes. Fingers
grip the grain. Dirt feathers at the push of the blade.
The arm sends bursts of power when he tells it.

Category 5 - Brodie Herndon Memorial - 1st Place

Vigil
Erin Newton Wells

for J, in the Covid Unit ICU

Often I am up before the light.
I see you leave or return,

depending on the shift or circumstance,
the ritual of putting on or taking off

garments worn to keep them safe
at home or where you go,

a place I cannot truly comprehend
from outside, knowing you enter

corridors of tragedy to give them
everything you can, then lose.

Often I am still awake at night.
I hear the wheels go by,

a whisper in the street, saying, hush,
and know you must have ways

by now to put the images aside,
or else you cannot go on,

the burden too great, their faces,
their last words, the way the others

plead with you to keep them here,
to make a miracle, if you can.

Category 5 - Brodie Herndon Memorial - 2nd Place

Blueberry Hill
Catherine West Johnson

Mother and Dad slow dancing
on the living-room carpet. Pops

swinging the quarter notes.
Lillian and I marching around

the room blowing paper horns.
We don't know

Larry Colburn
Hugh Thompson

and Glen Andreotta
are about to rescue Bo Da,

an eight-year-old boy hiding
under his mother's corpse.

Glen takes the chopper down.

Hugh vaults out. *What's going on here?*
Hugh demands. *Just following*

orders, Lieutenant Calley replies.
Hugh shouts to his crew. *Cover me!*

Shoot the bastards if they open fire.

Larry swerves his gun around
on a blue-eyed American soldier.

Off to bed, girls, Mom

commands. Hugh carries
Bo Da to the helicopter,

Larry lifts him up, Glen shifts
the throttle – they ascend

into a cloud – the ditches below coursing
with blood – a river running

from the head to the mouth.
My loose tooth falls out

and I put it under my pillow
hoping the tooth fairy

ups the ante this time and leaves
me more than just one quarter.

Mother reads us *Good Night Moon*
and as I fall asleep I can hear

Dad singing "Blueberry Hill"
in the living room.

Category 6 - Nancy Byrd Turner Memorial - 1st Place

Clearcut (A *Clogyrnach*)
Elizabeth Spencer Spragins

We log this land, then lay her bare
And singe her verdant maidenhair.
Eagles with no bed
Circle overhead,
Mourn their dead.
A wolf's lair

Retains the acrid scent of fear,
And phantom heartbeats echo here.
Slaughtered spruce and pine
Broken at the spine
Intertwine
In a bier.

The bones of woodlands make no sound,
But something rumbles underground.
Lightning's arrows fly,
Blind the daystar's eye,
And untie
What roots bound.

Now rivulets of vengeful rain
Abrade the earth from bald terrain,
Press their fingers deep—
Roots no longer sleep
Along steep
Ridge's mane.

The furies fettered to the rock
Within a buried prison block
Rattle chains in rage
Simmered for an age,
Crack their cage,
Snap the lock.

They pry the cliff face from her wall,
And when the landslide casts a pall
Demons brag of brawn.
Darkness swallows dawn,
Fissures yawn,
And we fall.

~Fones Cliffs, Richmond County, Virginia

Category 6 - Nancy Byrd Turner Memorial - 2nd Place

Signs and Wonders (English sonnet)
Erin Newton Wells

The board is not so simple as it seems,
a piece of wood she sanded at the edge,
the time it took to brush it off and clean
what dust she made, to lean it on a hedge
out front, a bit of help to haul it there,
the sky-blue paint she chose, cerulean,
a word she liked, the work, the extra care
to paint an earth in green, not let it run,
or how *Repair the World* in letters said
a thing she did to paint away the words
a vandal smeared so that they rudely read
another way, the pair of peaceful birds
she placed to contradict a damaged sign,
a work of art. And she was only nine.

Category 7 - Cenie H. Moon Prize - 1st Place

A Mantle of Words
Erin Newton Wells

*– Anna Akhmatova, whose poems became
a chronicle of the Stalinist reign of terror*

Please. You must be brief. She writes the lines
on a scrap. Read it quickly. Commit it to mind.
Give it life as you breathe. Now burn it.

The stove opens its mouth. Paper is ash.
The lines live as you say them over and over.

Carry them into the streets of Leningrad, boots
crunching hard crusts of snow until her words
become the pulse for those who cannot speak,
cannot breathe, who lie behind iron gates
or in their graves and cannot tell you of the terror
in this *terrible ghost* that pretends to be a city.

Paper is death. Remember. Keep it as litany
whispered ear to ear so quietly even the pigeons
brooding in the broken walls cannot hear.

Pass it one to another, her requiem of their lives,
like the legend of the mother, her cloak spread
over the people until safe to say their names
once more. Mantle of whispers and ash. *Ritual
beautiful and bitter.* Her words, a reliquary.

Category 7 - Cenie H. Moon Prize - 2ⁿᵈ Place

Luminosity
Chapman Hood Frazier
(To Deborah)

In this understory of hedgerow, a luminous
scansion, a meter
between shadow and light   and for an instant

morning stitching   the ridge top
                        till it sparks an explosion
of goldfinch   from the front field.

I followed you there   your hair
iridescent   in under glow
fated
when the light was right.

By evening   time's three-noted thrush call
sacrificed each scent   in fire

of memory   in starlight.

Category 8 - Judah, Sarah, Grace, and Tom Memorial - 1st Place

Didactic Haikus
Richard L. Rose

Impulse must not lead—
no Jeroboam mind-set:
Judah left alone—

Nor should rivalry—
Sarah's enemy cut off:
returned, a simoom—

Nor should grievances
(instead of grace) erect walls
of legal standing,

Nor cold *Summations*—
Calvin's, Tom's—come to replace
kind invitations.

Impulse, rivalry,
summing debts and grievances
shun serenity;

shut eyes; clamp the heart—
shaking its lobster-pot.
Winter is no home.

Category 8 - Judah, Sarah, Grace, & Tom Memorial - 2nd Place

Where the Ground Weeps
Erin Newton Wells

Babi Yar Memorial, Kyiv, dedicated Oct 6, 2021

As if pulled from earth, a dark wall of coal rises.
Water seeps on its face. Rest your head.
Place your hands against death.

You are meant to feel how cold. It does not move,
made and pressed from this very ground.
You cannot pretend not to see.

Knobs of quartz jut out. Teeth. Monster. Or prayer
to prod you toward these souls, stones
at the height of brow and heart.

The ravine lies under your feet. No mantle of soil
can hide where they burned. Look,
as through a camera.

Look, as through a tunnel of time, a tiny hole
bored into a rock, a scene from that day,
the earth riven, clothes scattered.

Those who wore them are flown, their bones lost,
their names vanished. Listen,
in case the wind knows.

Here, ten columns of steel, pierced with more stars
than the sky. A commandment of bullets,
your face mirrored in them.

Their bodies are written with riddles, their breath
the autumn air, their names aloft.
Name them. Call them beloved.

(On September 29, 1941, Ukraine's holocaust began at Babi Yar, a ravine in Nazi-occupied Kyiv. Within forty-eight hours, nearly 34,000 Jewish citizens were shot and burned there. By 1945, 1.5 million had perished, including others considered expendable by the Germans.)

Category 9 - Ada Sanderson Memorial - 1st Place

Elegy, Because the Season Does Not End
Erin Newton Wells

You hear it first, the memory of weather. Geese announce
in their awkward voice. Click of stiff legs

of the beetle slows in garden rubble. It searches for a place
to sleep. I find it when I dig the summer under,

sleek black sarcophagus where roots of melon linger.
No one tells it winter may not come,

or not as before, less need for long slumber and less cold.
The almanac shows its rows of tiny moons,

hunter and harvest, named for a time we barely remember,
time to sow or reap, all earlier now, or later,

as warmth stays on. Whatever burrowed, whatever flew
wakes or returns to a season begun too soon,

already underway without them. A few blue days, the haze,
a bare hint of chill, then much like before.

No snow last year, no snow for now, as it should. Hickory
throws down hard mysteries

for scavengers to gather. No one told them the rush is off,
that time slips from its chart, and the almanac

does not know. Cover the garden, brown leaves and straw
for those who sleep in hollows of silence.

Geese go on and on above the world in elegant arrows,
as if this is not so.

Category 9 - Ada Sanderson Memorial - 2nd Place

Earth to Earth
Gloria Williams Tran

I spied him on the glistening snow,
lying on his back, his claws curled
inward, his legs reaching for the sky.
I trudged through the snow to examine
this victim of a rare winter freeze

too frigid, too snowy for a robin to dig
in hardened soil for worm or slug.
His breast more brown than red,
laced with delicate white scallops,
his deepest underbelly pure white.
Beak pointed skyward, strong and straight.

Feathers soft to my touch as I caressed
him in my palm, willing him to revive,
to live again. His eyes, shrunken
within their sockets, glazed over,
gave no reply.

Mourning this silent songbird, I recalled
when the sun shone after the rains.
Robins gathered in my yard, celebrating
a feast of worms escaping flooded burrows.
Had this robin been one of them,
now returned to a remembered
place of worms and warmth?

When earth began its thaw, I dug a hole
in clay soil that yielded to my spade,
the ground soggy with melted snow.
The pit soon filled with muddy water.
At the funeral and burial, a scarlet
cardinal sang from a sycamore,
his tune piercing the air.

I lowered the robin into his watery grave
and shoveled the clumps of clay
over his body, remembering
other times when handfuls of soil
were tossed on caskets in solemn ritual.
My duty done, I marked the spot
with a heavy stone.

Category 10 - Charlotte Wise Memorial - 1st Place

Easter Morning
Chapman Hood Frazier

Mourning dove in the distance and on the feeder a cardinal.
The grass still wet and each breath visible. This is how endings
begin, a few wisps of clouds going soft on a clear blue sky
and the sun rising behind yellow-green poplars, pines thick
with pollen and gold.

These are the small gods I've grown used to. The tapping
of a flicker among the pines, a muffled bark beyond the rise
where dust lingers still from some truck's passing. This is
faith felt not from a rock rolled from the tomb's door
but in a breeze that bends the reeds by the creek's edge,

a whisper you wake to in the sound of your breath
in the pre-dawn dark. Each word, though, a misnomer
for love in the suffocating smoke of divorce, that smolders
still in the corners of the room. All desire eventually ends
in an abandoned tomb or in the spring's early blooms

remembered. Earth turns light again this year
lengthening each shadow through distance and slow time.
Each name carved in stone turns to flesh again. Each
sacrifice emerges in an owl's call before first light or
a word whispered in the ear from the dead before waking.

Memory layers each season's weathering towards bone
or at least the feel of it against skin. Each promise felt
from the tomb is a word revealed in this landscape's
grammar, something seen or felt in root and rhizome,
sense and sound, rising again to ripen and decay.

Category 10 - Charlotte Wise Memorial - 2nd Place

Home Studio
Meg Eden
after National Geographic's Photo Journal: April 2014

Those faux flowers
in a Shanghai wedding photo studio,
backdrop Versailles
under a leaking water pipe,
lumped hydrangeas pinned to the wall—
ones my mother might buy
to give the house life, like those plastic
wisteria garlands she bought
to wrap around our old porch columns,
peeling eggshell paint reddening
with rusty wounds,
to make us look civilized, she said.
As civilized as a graveyard—
those browning tea-stained flowers
left at headstones,
plastic stamens popping out.
She tried to grow real wisteria once:
waited six years then dug it up
when nothing blossomed.
Only then did she hear
it takes seven years
to see wisteria bloom & maybe that's what
my mother sees in fake things:
the same thing the Chinese girl sees,
sitting in a staged gold chair
& modern white dress, content
that the hydrangeas look real enough,
that the hydrangeas can be moved
from room to room & need no
roots or maintenance to stay
beautiful & young. That in this
man-made scene she too
can be briefly made eternal.

Category 11 - Robert Sergeant Memorial - 1st Place

City Birds
Norma Cofresi

By the side of a leafless country road,
a wake of turkey buzzards convenes to dine.
Are city birds any more civilized than country feathered fiends?
In New York City, pigeons pinch warm, salted pretzels from careless hands,
steal day-old bread from wrangling wrens, leave droppings to dry on sidewalks.

Tree-lined streets host flocks of birds in operatic testimonial
to life amidst cement, steel, bricks, and city noise,
a lulling counterpoint to thumping feet on asphalt playgrounds,
squeaks of a genuflected bus as it opens its doors,
screechy, discordant notes in an urban background symphony.

Humans talk and walk indifferent to the surround sound
or the jabbering of birds above their heads, or echoing noises
bouncing off walls, streets, trucks, and other people.
A red-tailed hawk scoops and hooks a running rat in its claws.
Sirens camouflage its victory caws freezing a feral cat out of a meal.

Black birds circle nine tall buildings atop a hill
in a pre-programmed dance, a rite of spring.
Geese honk and chase drivers walking toward parked cars.
Birds nest in nooks tucked under elevated trains
feeding their hatchlings popcorn, pizza, or burger remains.

An abandoned nest in the crook of a tree survives wind and rain.
In lowland parks, mallards in emerald parade, ducklings in tow.
In the cracks of a stone wall, hummingbirds feed on a flowering purple vine.
Country and city birds and people encoded to survive, to mate,
reproduce and feed their young. The concertos of life and death go on.

Category 11 - Robert S. Sergeant Prize Memorial - 2nd Place

A Round of Robins
Denise Wilcox

A round of robins
Descended.
Plucked berries
From dried vines.
Sipped water
From a driveway puddle.
Searched for worms
On frosty grass.
Swooped to hollies
Offering shelter.
Begged a pileated
For just one grub.
Flirted with song
And wispy wings.
A round of robins
Made the best
Of a gray day
Together.

Category 12 - Anne Spencer Memorial - 1st Place

After My Husband Decides to Move in with a Woman He Met Last Week, I Take Myself Out to Lunch
Gail Giewont

Everyone else is waiting
for someone. Beside
the restaurant's outside seats
people swing pastel shopping bags.
Cars crawl past. Engines thrum.
That clutch of being alone. A man orders
a quinoa bowl with shrimp for his girl,
takes it to-go when she doesn't arrive.
Midsummer heat closes in
even under the awning, becomes
a second skin. Two women in the corner stab
at their salads. It seems like everything
might wilt. I order the special, sip cold water
from my glass. The waiter asks
if I'm still okay. I am.
Across the street, drills whirr.
Hammers hit irregular beats.
Plywood suggests a shape,
half-formed in the pouring sunlight.
Something new coming into being.

Category 12 - Anne Spencer Memorial - 2nd Place

Call it Coping, Call it What You Will
Mara Lee Grayson

In May 2008, Bryan Steinhauer, 22, was attacked at a bar in Binghamton, N.Y. and suffered brain injuries so severe that he spent more than three months in a medically-induced coma.

In May, I stuff an hourglass
with cotton gauze. June is unremarkable
but for its aching.

By July, I've grown scars like cigarette paper,
and August makes me think
of baptism, a ritual
I've never known. It surprises me
to see accordions
still smoking on my forearm.
Grief looks different to everyone, I suppose.

At the hospital, I think
about Vermont, where we could be instead.
The ski resort is empty and belted
cows stand still.

Once my friend flew off the Alpine slide,
separated from her sled, dragged
the unsupportive vehicle down
the mountain like a painful appendage, incredulous
at the betrayal
and bleeding from the knees.
I dug my sneakers into gravel and waited at the base.

Sometimes now I dream I'm lying,
choked up on the poem in my throat,
with meadow stretched
in all directions, bovine-freckled, smell of grass
and sparkling
in the spacious off-peak season sun.
Traumatic is the memory

that only skin remembers,
but electricity
runs beneath the skin of all of us,
even those with histories like ours.

If questions are illusions of cognition, we are experts
in castles of our making.
Remember we climbed high upon the battlement
and jumped
straight down into the library?
Our minds have tricked us into thinking
language can
put chaos into order.

Like a man awoken from a three-month coma.
Like a bleeding woman walking down a mountain.

Category 13 - Handy Andy Prize - 1ˢᵗ Place

Piccolo Practice
Elizabeth Spencer Spraggins

My cat sits entranced at my feet
And twitches his tail to the beat.
Crescendos of wails
In dissonant scales
Convince him a feline's in heat.

Category 13 - Handy Andy Prize - 2nd Place

Internal Combustion
Richard L. Rose

In your endocrine studies, you're taught
all the ways that the body can rot:
metabolically clean
when the mixture is lean,
but a clunker that stalls when it's not.

Category 14 - Alfred C. Gary Memorial - 1st Place

This Day the Sea Will Boil
Erin Newton Wells

The Texas City Disaster, April 16, 1947

It all begins with sun against the rim
of earth, the flat vermilion disk, a shroud

of haze to redden sea and sky before
it glides above the port where ships will move

and gulls will call. A picture comes to life,
a town, its streets and shops, these houses where

its people wake. They stretch and go about
their lives. And who would think apocalypse

lies near, these very ships and what they bear,
these bags and what they hold, the chemical

to spread on fields so crops will thrive, the bags
packed tightly in the hull. A paper bag.

A fragile shield. The wax and rosin mixed
to keep it loose. The tinder that it needs.

A spark, a wisp of smoke. The walls grow warm.
The ship becomes a bomb. A woman stirs

a pot of food, then through the door, the yard,
the pot still in her hand, her brood of hens

alive but stunned, their feathers gone. A man
who never missed a day is home this once,

his workplace now a scar. The many lost.
Their bodies wash ashore for days, and some

are never found, the heat intense, their lives
consumed, a radiance of burning air.

An anchor heavy as two tons is found
a mile away, borne upward by the blast

and launched. A town erased, a photo now,
its people folded into time. The sea

will boil and scorch the sky. The sun will melt
beneath a blackened rim to end the day.

Category 14 - Alfred C. Gary Memorial - 2nd Place

At the Back of the March on the Pentagon, 1967
Raymond Copson

The bus. The anxious, keening woman I see.
A trap, she cried. Keep away from the Pentagon.
They're going to kill us all. Bad trip, we thought.
Psychedelic drugs had come to campus that year.

At Lincoln's statue thousands gathered, students and
older, veterans even were there, a few.
A tuba, a guy dressed up in general's garb, waving a
model Air Force bomber. Speakers
droned on a while, and famous folksingers strummed.

I can't tell now what was said or sung. The trumpet I
recall, the sound that sent us on our march
over the lovely bridge. Strange quiet till chants began,
Get Out, Get Out of Vietnam.

The crowd so thick we stopped at times for rest.
Fall sun was warm, John's grave in the hill still green.
Then on we went, and soon the sun was glinting off
helmets of soldiers with guns and bayonets.

Long after, a neighbor told me over gin,
We would have shot, but ammo was kept reserved. Young
soldier, drafted, scared. He'd been there, he knew.
Perhaps I was wise to linger back as day waned
and tensions grew. The woman's dire warning nagged. A
promise made to take care then called me home.

The country was not with us then. Support
the troops we were told. The tide of war soon turned,
opinions shifted some. Yet the troops stayed on
for six long years, the war not done for two more.

A waste of time that demo? Divisive mistake? Such
things were said. But in the years before, our country
seemed at last to be moving ahead, however slowly, in
justice, freedom, and truth. The way was being lost.
We had to speak out. And speak again, so many times,
alas.

Category 15 - Laura Day Boggs Bolling Memorial - 1st Place

To Catch Their Extravagant Wings
Erin Newton Wells

Late summer in the flyway, as we called it,
the path went through our town,
a sudden burst of color on the bending necks
of weeds, tall froth of lace
or face of purple aster. They rested, currents
of air setting them down,
glimmers of yellow and copper, rare glints
of blue or green from farther south,
their wildly extravagant wings. We took them
in our nets as specimens for school,
unbearable to see them thrash in my hoop
or coax them into a jar
mercifully as I could, or pin them to a board,
the grade unwanted for this robbery
of the air as they traveled north and sought,
by some miracle, exactly the home
they remembered, exactly how fragile wings
would take them there.

Category 15 - Laura Day Boggs Bolling Memorial - 2nd Place

Yodel for My Brother
Laura Sweeney

In Kendall Young Park, my half-birthday in June
we waded across the river's spill bridge, jeans hiked,

climbed onto the choo choo's slick smokestack. I slipped,
nailed my chin hard, so hard blood oozed down my chin.

You ran back, sloshed across the bridge, found Mom who
searched the blue Malibu for first aid, fixed a butterfly

bandage, like when you fell from our climbing tree, and
all you could see were blue, orange, yellow, and green stars.

Now, where I run my finger, it's smooth, except for the ridge
that reminds me of the days when you could soothe my boo-boos.

Category 16 - Joe Pendleton Campbell Memorial - 1ˢᵗ Place

Asters Greet as They Pass While Faintly Smiling
Cherryl Cooley

It is an unvoiced conversation we –
the Mom and I – never show or tell at real

family gatherings, our artful, cool,
collected, grinning faces hide what we –

and I – say to ourselves about what we left
of our souls at weeknight dinners or school,

what brooked in me when first we
both knew my muted voice would lurk

on the brim of quiet, choosing to be late
for chinwag, instead writing what we –

I should have said – in small diaries (*strike
through feelings; the wit, keep straight*)

I die a million times not speaking. We
mask the cycles of scarring, clothe thin

wounds beneath rivers of seersucker gin.
Her griefs are drunken versions of me. We

shriek a blues that imitates the bop in jazz,
dress our words for bitter winter in June.

I want to ask, but won't, what asters we
need to bloom before fall – *before we die,*

and when, and if, and how – *or soon.*

Category 16 - Joe Pendleton Campbell Memorial - 2nd Place

Badlands
Maggie Dillow

Sometimes the past brings trains to me first—all metal and standing too close to the tracks, baby teeth coated umber from the

chocolate bought at Ogilvie, once a year around Christmas. My own sticky fingers mechanically picking at skin tingling under

white tights, cheeks rouged with lipstick, dressed up and stirred by steel. Even then the city proper felt loud and other. I imagined

myself moving toward it, growing in and out of bright red lipstick, walking through malls packing cigarettes against my upturned

palm so everyone could hear. I was hot metal, an ancient skyrise fishing for shorts outside gas stations, lighting them up with stolen

pink Bics, putting them out in the soft earth and swimming naked in Lake Michigan, puffs of frosty breath expiring into mouths.

I was loving on empty, in the garage with a toothache, wondering what to wear. I was pink and splayed like the East River interstate I

would see for the first time ten years later, six months before Christmas or maybe after. I had no lake there. So I buried a rock—

basalt, coerced first as liquid and pressed not gently and without sound through crust from the center, from the celebrations there

and stories, beneath some sagebrush somewhere—where whatever is not light is like the kind that blood fills between skin and distal

bone—a rock made smooth by the *large lake* eight hundred miles East, where my mother brought us sometimes to watch the sunrise

before work, in a lab coat with the stethoscope in its pocket and polaroid pictures of holes in bodies. Wounds live lives, too. You can tell by their seasons—infected viridescent pits turned white-rimmed healing craters. I wasn't supposed to look, but she was

notably pleased with my strong stomach, never so much as a flinch, veering in at the photographs, careening to see—unlike the

cautious way you might approach a cliff's edge—soaking up lacerations and new, healthy stomas, a tethering taken for granted, like rocks cropped close to edelweiss, the heated minerals a home they didn't ask to be. Nurse, *nourish*. I thought the burying might

move time the way moving place moves people to do things like bury a rock hoping it might move time—like quartz ticking time

on wrists or the time I fell asleep on the train. Somehow—it was January and I was tired of telling time near the city. I wanted new

seasons where the sun came and if you ever wake up in a desert you'll know how the sun came and if you won't, well, there is

barely any room for the water to pool. The cracks in the earth as thin and dark as the space blood fills between skin and distal

bones—flicker of warm, worn ankles unfolding, staccato and cudgeling across land that is mostly sky, given little to rain.

Category 17 - Dr. Lucile E. Thompson Memorial Award - Technology - 1st Place

Ode for The Virtual Communities I Have Zoomed with This Year
Laura Sweeney

in Michigan & Arkansas & California,
Iowa & Oklahoma & Kentucky,
Colorado & Alabama & Minnesota...
all these states have been good company.

Yes, I'm in southern Illinois, but this is where
I live, not my community. I have connected,
plugged in with believers and nonbelievers,
democrats and republicans. How to describe them?

The woman who wrote about Proverbs 31,
I love your hats; the man with the relaxed
west coast style; the southern woman who
writes murder with a side of sweet tea;

the punk rocker Joy Rose and her bright
pink lipstick; and so many ordinary folks
who I want to tell thank you. Despite this
crisis and our collective fatigue you pivoted,

provided this kind of hospitality. Thank you
for our check-ins from naming a favorite food
I crave or restaurant I miss to how I am
preparing for winter. You have weathered

the ups and downs with me these months
and I've not been alone traveling coast to coast
when there is no way I could otherwise afford
the food or lodging or registration or gas.

You offered so much more: kindness.

Category 17 - Dr. Lucile E. Thompson Memorial Award - Technology - 2nd Place

An Underwood No. 5
Erin Newton Wells

Weight is what I think of, weight requiring heft to lift.
    Once placed it does not move, holds fast,
        load stone at which I type,

given by my father, exactly like his. He says I play
    the piano. I can play this. Like on the studio
        upright in my room, heavy

as the world, both hands pounding keys to push down,
    making music or words. The smell of metal
        is what I think of,

cast iron frame, ink, a tape rolled spool to spool. Bars
    of letters smack the page, jam, are pried,
        my fingers inky.

Gutenberg is what I think of, his alphabet on slugs,
    first printed page of *John*. I think of monks
        lettering by hand, works beautiful

and full of curling animals. My two sheets of paper,
    carbon between, fast and twice as much,
        though no animals. Miracle of metal.

Lever, pulley, wheel. Portable science of printed word.
    At my first newer keyboard, someone cautions,
        Gently. Don't kill the poor thing.

Too much muscle. In my first apartment the ceiling
    fell and broke the furniture. The Underwood
        stood firm, usable.

(First offered in 1900, Underwood's No. 5 was called the first truly modern typewriter, considered the most advanced technology of the day for portable writing machines.)

Category 18 - Elizabeth J. Urquhart Memorial, A Sense of Place - 1st Place

Ghosts Lights of Saratoga
Erin Newton Wells

Listen with an ear close to the way vowels
rise and fall on this flat coast in the crest line
of old growth trees, a slow whine, the way
they sing in a thicket of sluggish creeks,
swamps, really, the white bone of truth hidden.
He will set it to music if you want,
our local pundit, one foot on a rail of the porch,
guitar strummed like a lullaby so you sink
into the story, his tune a simple boat.
His children run wild as chickens, their voices
pulled by the moon rising now in violet dusk,
heavy air, fireflies, mosquitoes, our bare arms
and legs vulnerable, minds vulnerable
to where a story leads us.

If you go into the thicket at night, he says,
you might see it, a certain place on the road,
the light, a signalman who looks
for the head he lost when the train wrecked.
Or maybe other spirits, unfinished history,
tales in need of telling out past Silsbee,
Kountze, Vidor, Jasper. It used to be
the Sante Fe line to the Saratoga oil fields.

I wanted to go there. My father said no,
things lurk along a road like that at night.
It could be swamp gas, or headlights
from the highway nearby. Later I learned
it could be ghosts where men found
how long a branch can hold them
from the ground, or how a truck might
drag them until they felt the ground no more.
It could be the philosopher with his lantern,
looking for someone to listen to the truth.

Category 18 - Elizabeth J. Urquhart Memorial - 2nd Place

Visiting Danny
Kathryn Paulsen

After dinner in the Soo, with lock view,
we watch the ore boats, a thousand-footer,
a six-hundred-something footer,
an hour of free entertainment.
The crowd of tourists and locals shout questions to the crew—
Where do you come from? Where are you bound? We gaze
into the slowly setting sun, remembering
that Danny worked on an ore boat one summer.

Not till after dark, in the car
on the way to not-quite-home,
do I find the moment or the words:
"It's been a long time
since I've visited Danny's grave."

"We drove right by it this afternoon,"
Dad says. "I said,
'There's Danny.'"
"I didn't hear you," I say.
"I wish I'd heard you."
And wonder now what else
I haven't heard.

Hard rain all night.
It's raining still. Dad speaks
of flowers ordered, the cemetery's offer
of flowers forever, for a lump sum.

"Be strong for your father," Mom said back then,
meaning, "Hold back your tears."
For a moment now, we stop holding back,
for him and for her.
Hug each other.
       Then
"Goodbye, Danny," Dad says,
as we head for the car,
as if we'd just sat
and talked a while
after saying hello.

Category 19 - The Joanne Scott Kennedy Memorial - 1ˢᵗ Place

Candle Flame
Claudia Serea

Long—

long—long—
short—

long—long—long—
trembling,

its yellow dress flickers
over soft cotton marrow.

The flame rises toward the ceiling,
a magic bird—*măiastră*—free,

but not free, feet tied,
cast in heavy paraffin.

I need to burn these wax boots, it says.

They weigh me down,
and I don't need them in heaven.

Barefoot, I'll climb
on a prayer pinned to the moon,

stirring a black swirl of smoke,
dancing to my own music,

lit for the dead,
for the living, trembling,

long—long—long—
short—

long—long—
long

Category 19 - The Joanne Scott Kennedy Memorial - 2nd Place

Fish Eyes
Kaitlyn Graham

I wondered if you were suffocating
under his blue t-shirt I draped over your tank.
I know fish don't breathe light. If they *could*

he and I would have killed you a dozen times, Ed.
Starved you of seeing what we do in bed when
not even fish are watching. I'd cover your eyes

with my hands if I could, like my mother would
during sex scenes in R-rated movies. Emily
the Catholic neighbor said fifth graders shouldn't

watch rated-R movies, but when her more-Catholic
mother left the room she begged me to tell her
what sex looks like. She spent the summer

before middle school wearing her Communion cross
necklace, twirling in the mirror whispering, "Wearing
this…wearing only this" in her nightgown.

How do we look skin to skin devouring each other?
Two figures smashed together like that; my body
more naked, *more* twisted than ever.

When he left, and it was just you and me, I'd lift
your t-shirt veil to open your eyes, and together
we'd breathe the quiet light of a dark room.

Category 20 - Honoring Fatherhood Award - 1ˢᵗ Place

All the Whens
Stacy Clair

When I was young I was very ill
You worked a ton to pay all the bills

When your divorce was imminent you fought for full custody
And went into debt just to hold onto me

When you bought that new car you took me for the first ride
We didn't have to go far as long as I was by your side

When the blustery winter made it unbearable in our old home
You moved our only heater into my room alone

When I was fourteen I wanted to play the guitar
You bought me one that shined and gleamed and said I'd be a rockstar

When I became depressed during those teenage years
You refused to let me drown in my terrible fears

When I came home with pink hair and a metal bar in my tongue
You didn't glare or make me regret what I'd done

When you saved some money to buy that little boat
You took me tubing and skiing then we'd cut the engine and just float

When I decided to marry a man I told you smiling with glee
You willingly gave him my hand as long as he'd take care of me

When we filled our home with rescue pups instead of grandkids
You gave them just as much love as my husband and I did

When I called nine-one-one in the early morning light I knew you'd be gone by that night
You told me not to put you in the ground or I'd feel guilted to visit a lot year round
So I'm headed out to sea one last time
It's just you and me in the waves and sunshine

I'm spreading your ashes hoping the water will mirror your face
Tears falling from my lashes I leave you in your final resting place
I hope you'll visit me every once in a while
And stop by in my dreams with your big Dad hug and a smile

Category 20 - Honoring Fatherhood Award - 2nd Place

Breakers
David Patteson

>We'd wade out
>Flanking him, taunting,
>Splashing, and daring while
>He would mock plead for mercy
>Then duck under and swim straight out
>Into the deep, more certain than
>A homing turtle.
>
>We ventured only as far as the breakers
>Fighting their foamy slaps
>Till with salt stinging eyes, and seashell ears
>We stumbled ashore
>And collapsed onto our towels.
>
>We'd sun dry and watch him
>Slow crawl across the ocean horizon
>Relentless as the waves, till we'd grow bored
>And wander the boardwalk with our allowances.
>We'd always return to find him on the towel
>Reading some dog-eared paperback.
>
>We'd charge him
>squirting our water guns,
>Climbing over his shoulders and then whine,
>"We're hungry, we're bored.
>Let's…"
>On land he was helpless—
>Against our relentless, persistent attacks,
>he'd always break.

Category 21 - Ekphrastic Poetry Award - 1st Place

The Rose Window
(for Campbell)
Chapman Hood Frazier

Suspended above the nave
a morning glory   of light
diffusing green along the floor

as it washes the apse
a violet blue   white
beams   searchlight
across the floor

and I remember
my last flight   over Dresden
trailing thunder   praying
the night stay dark enough
to hide in

now   praying here too
for our salvation   my child
in a circle of light
no bigger than   your face

blonde hair   hands
clasped   above your head
as you dance   dancing

in perfect circles.

Category 21 - Ekphrastic Poetry Award - 2nd Place

world of woe
Rich Follett

I am a poor
       wayfaring stranger…

a fine song, yes,
but this is no song:

this is
my actual *life* –
all that i have,
all that i know.

my left foot is
a timid, darting
furtive mouse, dainty but
forever fretful;

my right,
plodding and flustered,
is a tortoise
tracing palsied curlicues
in the dust to which
i will soon return.

these decrepit oddments,
these trappings,
are my crumbs and my carapace –
together, they determine
whether progress or death
rules the day.

you are green, traveler.

you look to me for answers?

i have none.

the way is hard,
will always *be* hard;
i look back
only when looking forward
cancels breath.

this world is weary and
we who wander
only grow wearier…

left foot, mouse;
right foot, tortoise:

any minim of release
lies in knowing
which foot to use
and taking one

more

step.

The Wayfarer – Hieronymus Bosch

Category 22 - Emma Gray Trigg Memorial - 1st Place

To Uncertainty
Jay Udall

You're in the other shoe
waiting to drop, the approaching
hurricane's trajectory—
you unseal the box
of anxiety's bright knives—
pick the lock in the chest
of fear at 3 AM—you're here—
not here—the void in the flesh
of thought, the opening
edge—what comes next—
outcome of the story—
game, campaign, medical test—
the timing and details
of our deaths. We offer
prayers, plans, pills, programs—
gambits, guesses, bets—you give
only the moment, all there is—
a blue and green kite rippling
in a passing window's sky—
a goldfinch on a tree of heaven's branch
leaping off—

Category 22 - Emma Gray Trigg Memorial - 2nd Place

Blue Peony
Peter C. LaBerge

We didn't know it then, but already
we had begun our version of opening:

ultra-violet in the wind-wound
June. Here we were, Columbus

again. Sunday: blueberry pancakes
in bed. Again, bells pollinating

morning with music: sidewalk
worship, milkcrate drum. We knew

no god, but we opened the windows
in the kitchen anyway. *Blue*

on the seed packet, ultra-violet
& terrified upon opening. *Boys*,

boys queered upon opening—
years ago, not yet anyone

to each other, in basements
separated by whole states. Muting

our buzzing TVs—only once
we were sure

everyone around us was asleep. Then,
touching ourselves—watching

the men we dreamt of loving
as they mouthed whole scenes

we knew by heart—watching
these men & that love

assembling, then disassembling
into gray snow. Later, still

strangers to each other, we'd rinse
the taste of first love from our mouths

with day-old water. Even once,
years later, we'd opened—
in the same yard, such luck—
even after shared hesitance,

even now…I still catch myself
expecting blue.

Category 23 - Karma Deane Ogden Memorial - 1st Place

Hydrangeaphilia
Gail Giewont

"...plants retain the blossoms until they shatter, which can occur as late as winter." --diynetwork.com

My shears shape you
into a form of longing.

The earth's acid
changes your expression,

makes you blush
or grow cold.

But it is the cold of you
I love best,

sky echoing in your blossom,
soft petals of sorrow unfolding.

Open your many faces,
blue moons blinking awake.

Time and snow will weaken
your flowers to glass.

When winter leeches you fragile,
let me be the one to break you.

Category 23 - Karma Deane Ogden Memorial - 2nd Place

Jig
Cherryl Cooley

For Gregory Hines and all the men who are hoofers in their daily lives

Men with guts for eyes say to me about the dance that feet
should always make a mark, kick simple dirt, press
down to fend for the body's frisky cage, keep time,
kick the nylon donkey rut, get in a face, show some vein,
crack the nonsense, whop a nut, end and mean, like a soul –
not in your hands, or in a cup, not as a rage of needy skin,

but as a man, a *him-do-come, him-then-go*, who skins
a lie to tap a truth, who, empty-handed, drags his feet
(some days aloof) to hangdog altars for vulgar pay, a soul
who dances anyway. Nicked-up, ding-down shoes press
freakish into dirt-nail blues. *What a man must keep in his veins,
say in his sleep, water down, explain.* Do I believe in time?

(*It ain't mine.*) It's not the backfire of heels, the whack of toes. Time:
An order: Bang from the bones to sing a psalm beneath the skin,
and in your teeth, an antsy fang; in your arch, a plucky vein.
Be *in* and *on*. Spank tough on thuggish days. In brutish ways, the feet
will blister roads, buck timbered floors, and in the cyclic press
of tripping doors, where dreams turn quickly into cysts, there is soul,

a man in full ghost. No hocus-pocus stooge, I dream in fists. My soul
a lenient wish, rubber heeled in hard-knock glue. I'm time out of time,
before its time, shoe-scuffed shoe. I ride the ridge of a dirty dime, press
luck into my hair. I give off smell. I'm spicy smoke in salt fresh skin.
Ish! My dance is an honorable sin. I scavenge air. Away – out of vein –
far from a poor house. Stepping keeps me sane. Is gravy in my feet.

Keeps me honest and rude, one long-body daisy chain of feet
and other limbs tricked out. Unglued. Big bean, boodle, soul:
I grind. Gut noodle in doubt, I do-or-die the same – in the vein
of anyone who's had to prance the teeth, beg and borrow time,
swallow, skim, crawl and climb – *flit* – sun and sambo in the skin.
Good sweat means more of it – just around the bend. I press

forward or reverse, thump memory, snitch regret, crave the press
of softness against this dream, lesser fret for haggard feet,
fatted schemes to ensure I eat. To the backbiters: *Skin* –
a healthy ration of muscle and spine. To the rooters: *Soul* –
the fever of hard-nosed hustle, of loose legs and taut time.
I'm here to seduce, tether blood to a pulse, drag your veins.

I shake loose from this skin, weather the white-hot press
of forerunning men who worked their feet, blessed my veins,
perked this beat – *sweet soul Mary Jane!* All in uncaged time.

Category 24 - Loretta Dunn Hall Memorial - 1st Place

Rose Tea
Erin Newton Wells

I broke the cup and everything spilled out
the way the sun rose that day and rose
until too bright to tell where light left off

because I could not look, blinded.
It fell away in curves, rocked and went still,

all of it smooth. A cream bisque inside
when held up, each piece drinking light
then letting go, remembering

or forgetting clusters of poppies around
the outer bowl, their dark eyes,

their feathery leaves, narrow rim of gold
for the lip. It would be thin tea,
rose hips, dried peel of orange in steam.

Here, love, you would say, *the scent first*,
and offer it as prophesy.

In pieces now, but the ring of porcelain
still whole where your finger held the cup.

I will not mend it with the art of gold dust
in glue. The scent is here in the color
of poppy, orange and rose.

What was lifted by a mother's hand is here.
On the delicate foot, tiny lettering, a potter
in England, saying we belong somewhere.

Category 24 - Loretta Dunn Hall Memorial - 2nd Place

Namesake

Chapman Hood Frazier

A cornflower in a lapel, and by the garden gate overhung with white roses the dead boy watches.
Some afternoons he sits in front of the gas heater with an eyeless dog. He does not speak.

The old woman next door gives pennies in his name, shiny pennies, if I look both ways before crossing the street he died on.

She waits for me by the curb. Her wire-rim glasses glint in sunlight. She leans forward on a rake handle to watch as I cross. Pennies bright in her hand.

A mother sings a lullaby in the rocking chair. A peace rose glows in the bud vase. She remembers
her dead brother. By evening, one white petal lies on the mahogany table.

Downstairs, an apron hangs in the broom closet. Grandmother washes the baby's spoon with his initials and in the attic's secret room a lamb lies on its side stitched with his name in blue.

After everyone is in bed, I go downstairs to the music room. He is lying on his back in moonlight
by grandfather's brass elephant beside the hearth.

The blue flame of the gas heater gutters softly as I bend close. From my pocket, I take a shiny penny and place one on his open eye, then the next. He whispers our name.

Death comes in February. Bare trees, scattering of dry snow along the walk and in the wind, a few dry leaves scutter beneath the hedgerow. The sound of a truck passes outside in the dark.

No stars. Clouds smoke the cold scud of sky. Trees hold their crystalline breath in this
the dying time. Someone upstairs whispers my name.

Category 25 - Undergraduate Poetry Award - 1st Place

On a Sidewalk
Alexander Lazarus Wolff

The people rush around me as they head to work.

People with some place to go pass me by,
entering the embassy.
               And I…
                                   these clothes I inhabit,
this flesh of mine, this serviceable body that the world
goes by but never sees…. A businessman peers
from the Chrysler Center skyscraper, split off
from the world by a tinted shade of glass, concealed
by that which allows him to see. Each window possesses
a life, all these deep-dyed windowpanes. And, behind them,
a man who types away at his desk; two others bantering
around a watercooler. Inattentively, passively, and far-
off, dozens of pale faces stare, watching
the day glide by like old newsreel.

The people and traffic increase around me
like floodwater flowing over a dam. A woman
bumps my arm; car horns blare like warning sirens.
And I stand still, letting the onslaught rush around me.

Category 25 - Undergraduate Poetry Award - 2nd Place

Apathy
Ian Garrabrant

The most dangerous facet
of my depression,
that omnipresent addiction
to imprecision and inconcision.
Lurching forth to infect any lingering speck
that lacks its natural air
of circumspect inaction,
never asking what or where;
only why
should I expend a modicum of effort,
or a moment's attention,
when ultimately there is no dissension,
no time left for repentance,
on our march to oblivion?
That growing why lays siege the mind,
yearning for an answer that breeds satisfaction,
not sated, it detaches
no more to be stagnant,
attached to a question.
It presses advantage,
waylays every action or attempt at reflection,
dissecting their motives, starving
for just a single glimpse
of motivation.

Index

C

Clair, Stacy 48
Cofresi, Norma 27
Cooley, Cherryl 39, 58
Copson, Raymond 36

D

Dillow, Maggie 40

E

Eden, Meg 26

F

Follett, Rich 52
Forsbergh, Eric 2
Frazier, Chapman Hood 4, 5, 3, 18, 25, 51, 61

G

Garrabrant, Ian 63
Graham, Kaitlyn 47
Grayson, Mara Lee 30

H

Haile, Edward Wright 7

J

Johnson, Catherine West 4

L

LaBerge, Peter C 8, 55

M

P

Patteson, David 50